PARODIES
LOST

For Margie Ferguson,
with gratitude
for your
words, + hope
my verse lives
up in part—

ALAN POWERS

Alan Powers
westport, MA
winter Solstice
2016

Front cover art: Wordsworth, poet-pup
Back cover art: "Miss Paris, I love Paris…"
Book design by Justine Elliott

Cover art and illustrations by Susan Mohl Powers

For my students in Massachusetts community colleges and the University of Minnesota who energized my classes while often supporting their families, such as

Judy Mendenhall, flutist, **Darlene White**, comic Moth and music educator, **Mark Bisson**, singer-teacher, **Gary Earle**, attorney, **Marc Folco**, columnist, **Cassandra Hall**, promoter, **Michael Martins**, historical museum director, **Ron Potvin**, champion historical writer and museum director, **Scot Stets**, actor and videographer, **Mark Sardinha**, poet and plumber, **Chrisanne Souza**, poet and teacher, **Leslie F Uehara**, teacher (starting in Japan), **Tony Silva**, Japanese teacher, **Jeffrey Silva**, police spokesman, chief and attorney, **Jeff Majewski**, detective and teacher, **Joan Thomas, Susan Plaud, Sandra Stuart, Lisa Raposo, Joseph Brooks, Carolyn Swift, Victoria Passier, Omayra Fontanez, Don Gagnon** and **Erin Donahue**.

With a better memory, I could cite hundreds.

The first chapter of *Parodies Lost* was published in my collection, *Westport Soundings*, Westport, *MA 1994* under the title "The Poet Onagain (Lines for Pushkin)"

"He knew—from a picture of Rod McKuen—
of all his race, the poet makes
the saddest face. And next to a hound,
the saddest sound."

"Wordsworth, a reflective poet pup:
            'Of many words I have no need,
                    Like all those human lies—
            Say, where they've been. With one stiff sniff
                    I know, the noser knows.'"

            After Dylan Thomas:
"Love burst firth, froth on the sea
  Foams on the rolling, beating surf."

            Country Western:
  " I'm only a laborer
    In the Factory of Love;
    I been workin' ev'ry night
  And now the job is done.
    My wife, she made a baby,
    But I have been the one
    Workin' in the Factoree of Love."

"Better a beetle in a pile of dung
Than anything in a rapper's song."

POEMATIS PERSONAE

in order of appearance

Onagain	*the poet and parodist*
Miss Paris	*Onnie's early teacher*
Auntie Frieda	*Onnie's loyal supporter*
Eddy	*the homeless writer*
Cassie	*Aromatherapist, model*
Aura	*Cassie and Onnie's year-old*
Wordsworth	*the dog and writer*
Armand	*A full-time Academic*
Onagain's Dad	*Orphan, Navy vet*
The Author	*Wannabe Pushkin*

Parodies:
R. Herrick (75), E. Dickinson, D. Thomas, J. Ashbery (79),
Shakespeare, M. Angelou (81), R. Wilbur (84), Scarron, Yesenin,
Persius (86), Catullus (86). Pushkin, Wordsworth.

Onagain's Song

Epilog: Pushkinny Dipping

So, reader, now you know Onnie's Dad
Should be arrested, and his Auntie's
Sad scandals, though a harmless vice.
Here most everyone a writer is,
Even homeless Eddy and the dog
Wordsworth—doggerel, but in a league
With his namesake—though as for that, think
Of Cassandra multi-talented.
How will that turn out, their life in art
For a country that wants to see men
Throw balls, hit and run, and dive at hard
Grounders or backhand serves. Give us youth
Action flicks and MTV. For you,
Reader, pour some port and drink the truth.

I. Onagain Finds Himself

He knew— from a picture of Rod McKuen—
of all his race, the poet makes
the saddest face. And next to a hound,
the saddest sound.
                              He found despair
came hardest on a sunny day,
with a butch haircut. But in the rain,
bedraggled,
                        "Loneliness," he thought,
"has wet me through," and going in,
he wrote of going out again.
Though all alone, he never felt
at all poetic while he wrote.

No poet writes about a wife, so first
he got divorced and found a lover—
then gave up living with his mother
(of the order I'm not sure, but first one
and then the other).
                              Divorce regained
him time to write of psychic pain,
a subject read by all with pleasure.
But separation had its problems;
without a wife, he had to cook,
which never happens in a poem—
the poet standing, frying ham.

A Writer must be open to Experience.
One evening on Mt. Auburn Street
a head said, "Lemme smell ya feet?"
He did not laugh, but empathized,
identified with him, and said
"No, let me smell your feet instead,"
and this was willingly obliged.
What good are words— they are too weak
to express what he was feeling then—
but now he knows, as Writers must,
what's it like to be, in fact,
an olfacto-podiphobiac.

He was feeling low until
someone said they felt "depressed."
"Depression" made him feel much better.
Like a modern man, now he can see
psychiatrists, or buy a hat
on impulse like a house-bound wife.
Beyond— and more poetic yet—
lies "existential ennui."
                    That's caught
from reading Sartre. It cures the rest,
except there's just one cure for it:
ANGST.
            Once this word is known,
you'll never feel "depressed" again.
But no matter how he groomed
this sensation, ANGST, he felt
only in translation.

His hopes were dashed.

                                    Dispassionate,
he sought careers as a degenerate,
to train first as a deviate,
and work his way on up.

                                    Or down,
from "dropout" who's too bright to fit
the molds of formal education.
Since writers should know all, he bought
Encyclopedia Americana.
He started *Volume Twenty-Two,
Photography to Pumpkin.* That
title was symbolical, he thought,
and the story good— though lacking plot.

To relax the ANGST he almost felt
transactional analysts would help,
"to ease your mind, and even sometimes
improve your I.Q...."

                                    "No Thank You,"
the genius blanched, and searched a New
You, easy as a sunshine day
at Monterey, effortless as fastfood
or checkomatic instyservice.
Why waste years encrusting rusks of
barnacle wisdom? Try Esalen,
scientological transcendental
or snoozilogical meditation,
Rekkei, E.S.T. and Silva Mind
Control, Bioenergy and Zen...

To groom his Weltsmertz, his end
of the world jadedness, he went
deeper into drugs, from Mary Jane
to her expensive cousin Cocaine.
These buoyed and dropped him like a plane
in an air pocket.
                    For some weeks
he lived the life of many friends,
and left for no apparent reason.
He said, "Their mellow season is
ephemeral— and actually,
they didn't help my memory."

What is not ephemeral? you ask,
and I can only say what happened
next: Onnie searched his Identity,
with professional help, certainly,
who found his Ego, and his Id
(his Superego must have moved).
He learned of crises Oedipal
and fathers ineffectual,
of traumas since he'd had no kid—
and other traumas if he did.

It's important for this poem
that he find himself. Aren't you
concerned? I know that I am.

But would he ever Find Himself?
A distressing prospect, to be lost
among familiar places, not
to know the who who's doing what
you yourself do do.

              This quest
consumed his life from day to week,
who little wanted to become,
as David Copperfield had done,
a new you who's a Gentleman!

That surely had surprised him; still
less did he expect to awaken
as Pretender to the Throne of Spain.

He was worried by his bulging pot
and frankly chose to institute
the American self-discipline
and sacred regimen called Diet.
But to be convincing at that,
he also had to jog and trot
since simply walking wasn't frantic
enough, or enough athletical—
gone the days when it sufficed
to take a daily constitutional.
Dieting opened a world of friends
and Subject Conversational
to pursue when he exhausted

"Nice Day!" or Subject Meteorological:
When, and where, and how he'd lost
ten pounds, eating only grapefruit
and bananas, or avoiding meat.

When he found himself, he seemed
the same as he had always been;
hairy on his face, and lean
except his esophageal home
which was growing plump digesting
the bulk of his organic food.
Bean sprouts, chick peas, nuts and raisin
rice, and rice, and rice with chicken
organically raised, without a bit
of suspect feed inside of it.
Did he find the King of Spain?
An Artist? Or a Gentleman?
No. The same face filled the mirror,
with less hair, and slightly older.

II. Recess Exam and Eddy

Onnie had gone to schools that sorted
kids like eggs, on the nascent theory
that they'd all been born with certain skills;
the schools paid just to "place" and "track"
like genes, the lore of class or bloodline.
Yet democracy promoted this
as test assessment, standardized.
The gravest test he had not passed
first, when he transferred in third grade
to a new school.
                    Someone yelled, "Pig Pile!"
at recess and he was tackled, felled
with twelve fine fellows on top of him.
That was not the test, but when he'd run
to Miss Grimm, then he flunked Pig Pile One.

They, with the hearts of Caesars, pardoned
him, let him join either third-grade
softball team; the one lived cityside
in town, with long names like Farasian,
Zuccolo, Margolis versus Smith
and Douglas, Bennett. These all lived
in houses with more space around
them, or near cellar-holes that froze
in winter— A backhoe dreamer planned,
had dug these suburbs of his mind.

Onnie chose the easy names, then thanked
the fortune on his side, for Geez!
it turned out these
                    were the ones who won.
On's was the better team. They won
on balls hit almost foul, on calls
"Safe at Second!" on strikeouts where
they knew "He swung! He broke his wrists."

The game began about to be won,
continued being, ended having
won, inevitable as verb tenses.
But then he noticed the better team
played for the losers. He thought, How come?

His Sunday school deemed great loss was gain,
like Christ and Peter, or the pilgrims
that first winter. But Matt Margolis
was no martyr. He could pitch and hit
better than anyone on On's team.
Same went for the others, all better.
Onnie learned their secret, tried to join
the losers, who played semi-pro ball
years later.

Hit with litigation!
Argue ev'ry call. That's how they won.

A girl just out of college he first loved
in fourth grade, Miss Paris, his teacher.
And her name! Paris in the Springtime,
Paris in the Fall, April in Paris,
The first time I saw...

                     Two grades later,
first books he found and loved on his own:
they featured *Bomba the Jungle Boy*,
once in the Cave of Anacondas
while Lily Pons' operatic rills
fell from the classroom wall Intercom.
A lifelong debt to his "gifted class":
viz, sopranos sang like jungle snakes.

Cartoons supplied the antidote when
he studied opera with Bugs Bunny,
The Barber of Seville with barber's
chair periscoping like fire-ladder.
Films stole great music as did ads.
Of the thousands of Garfield stickers,
who knows who knew of the President
Garfield gave his name, unrequested.

As for used Coke bottles, Pepsi, beer,
he carried them in plastic bags
to leave at the Redemption Center.
Wasn't redemption a Christian wish?
Resolute, he found it in the trash.

The bearhunt in *The Yearling* gripped
him as his seventh grade teacher
read it aloud, half an hour a day—
Appalachian brush, the woods of Maine.
He soon learned the power of his pen
(from Latin *penna* for feather, quill).
This was by accident, his first poem
made his spinster teacher sad,
while he was just trying to rhyme
"Dreams of hope, of love for lovers/
Dreams of days long past for others."
The teacher, a Miss bless her, forgave
the bad rhyme, sentiment, clichés.

On had flunked Pig Pile One, but remained
in gifted sections: *Evangeline*
they read, right after Dick and Jane
because by fourth grade, it's *Tom Sawyer*,
Ancient Mariner by fifth, and then
Hamlet could be read by grade six, spring.
The School Psychologist approved, since
so many parents divorced. The Prince
resented his mother's remarriage,

just as did Onnie's sixth-grade peerage.
Some early aromas bedappled
his mind—crawling on floors newly waxed,
the smell in the rain of the sidewalk
as he sat on it protesting home
from the playground; his own sheets so cool,
blanket of wool acrid from mothballs
in the fall chill, percolating smell
of coffee bubbling on the wood stove,
the seep of kerosene from starting
the wet wood, that musk of damp woodsmoke,
the smell of pines, the dark woods of Maine,
and the fresh aroma of success—
the smooth red leather and new car scent.

The red seats of the fifty-eight Merc
Bathed in "Davey, Davey Crockett, King
Of the wild frontier…Raised in the woods
Till he knew ev'ry tree, / Kill't a bar
When he was just three / Davey, Davey"
went the refrain for guys who'd wander
the old woods behind suburban homes
where you could learn every tree, really
spindly maples, occasional oak,
often a painted turtle or skunk
and ferns! three feet high, like hallways
as some old poet said for always.

The radio blazed with candy-voiced girls
wanting guys, like "I will follow him /
wherever he may roam./ / There isn't
a mountain too high, / Nor an ocean
too wide (something) I will follow him."
Radio girls were ready; they waited
Just behind the speakers and the firewall
Of the Merc. Like pistons their desire,
like overhead cams their famous fear,
"Will you still love me tomor-uh-ow?"
Harder to field such bare, backseat fear;
easier to tame the wild frontier.

When Aunt Frieda came from Ohio,
she listened to a country station,
songs that took her far away from her
life to couples' stories, losses
mostly, but spunky singers like Cash,
or wistful Hank Williams, or that wry,

> "I'm only a laborer
> In the Factory of Love;
> I been workin' ev'ry night
> And now the job is done.
> My wife, she made a baby,
> But I have been the one
> Workin' in the factoree of Luv."

Frieda cranked it up, her favorite lines,

> "She has made a bayee-bee
> Now I know that she took me
> To work in her Factoree of Luv."

Auntie boogied in the kitchen to
the slide guitar, and the luscious drawl
"I'm happy at my job." That was all.

Speaking of dreamers and la-la land,
where was that Buddha-bellied fellow?
Eddie lived as a philosopher
like Diogenes, his tub his car.
Instead of the Great Alexander
asking what he could do for him,
the bright high-beams of the local cops
pull up behind, How could they serve him?
Because he could not remain right there.
He had not been sleeping, just resting
on his sleeping bag in the Buick
wagon with his boxed library stacks
beside him: Dickens' *Expectations*,
Joyce's *Portrait*, Toole's *Confederacy*,
a few more, which the campus police
scan suspicious with their truncheon lights.

"What's those?" "Books."
                                "They yours?"
                                        "Mine aren't published."
"They're *not* yours?"
                        "No, they're mine, though I
didn't write 'em. Tolstoy did, Dickens."
"Anything else here that's not yours?"
"No, don't you see? They're all mine, but I...

I was joking, 'cause I've written three
books—over here, in this box. See these."
"They don't look much like books."

"That's the way
books look before they're published."

"Yeah? Well,
You've still gotta move your vehicle."

III. Cassie, Sex and Realty

The eighties danced in, full of promise
like *Playboy* to a teen, see it shine
behind the counter, its pages reamed
with ads for amplifiers, filtered
cigarettes, Scotch, and automobiles
with black Naugahide upholstery
available through dealers.

                             The girls—
such accessories! They do not hide
their Naugas. They prefer their lovers
to sing them vintage Beatles lyrics,
one with pizzaz, "I once had a girl,"
tinged with wit, "Or should I say she once
had me"—or *not*

                        as the case may be

And, more often, is. Oh, amplify,
you bright Magazine Amplifiers,
our poor power to find such a girl.
Where's a truthful counselor, one who'll
tell you to your face, "Dude, forget it!
Those girls all live in L.A., New York
and Chicago. At least a thousand
miles separate you from the mere glimpse
of one. You'd have been better off not
to know of their waxy showroom sheen,
better t'have been born a Moslem teen."

Better, indeed, never to have heard
of Reagan, insider trading, junk
bonds, the "War on Drugs"—we surrendered—
the Iran-Contra scandal, Donald Trump,
deregulation...
                    that word alone
had ruined many Savings and Loans
because it opened the gates of greed.
A current of greed grew to a sea;
malls burgeoned like Dock on fallow land,
houses sprung like Crocuses, condos
filled sidehills with their storybook names,
Heritage Commons, Hudson-on-Thames.

"Cranberry Lane" and "Bayberry Drive,"
developers turned poets, naming,
naming. Realtor-poets keep the trees,
"Birch Lane" and "Hickory Road" they keep
but shun the legacies of Swamp Road,
Old Cemetery Hollow; Pine Hill
they keep, but deep-six Marsh Avenue,
Mosquito Pond Road, and Anthill Forks.
Onagain noticed that he had not
seen Tornado Lane, Flood Plain Street,
nor Town Dump Drive, or Cockroach Court.
Those were omissions, but intended,
surely. America had become
the land of the sales poem, jingles sung
on television, land of names,
new names for older games; hard callous

spokesmen did not talk of beggary
or Christian virtues like charity.
No, they regretted the rising homeless
numbers, but what could they do, pray tell?
In these boom times, any fool could see
'twas better to spend gov'ment dollars
on condos that taxpayers could sell
and realize profits. The homeless, well…

God bless America; rejoice, All,
that everyone you meet doesn't kill
you; America, be glad and sing:
thank God Dick Cheney's not your friend;
Fellow American, be glad and sing:
your auto's recalled before it maims
you; America, Land of the Free,
thirty-day, money-back warrantee;
Home of the Brave, of the guarantee.
Bless America, Home of the Cheese-
burger, Home of the stand-alone Home,
Home of the Realtor, Land of the Land.
Here you can save the life of a cat,
build a small mansion, be a pet vet.

Onagain grew a man of courage,
for despite warnings, braving death
from kidney failure or what's worse,
he took his tea with more than one
teaspoon of that known carcinogen,
sugar—although there are reports

he lost his nerve before the label:
"*Warning*: the Surgeon General
has determined that Diet Cola
can prove hazardous to your health.
Not recommended for pregnant mom
or for hypochondriacal men.
Drink only as directed— and when."

He met her after a cola binge,
"Cassandra, Cassie, my lassie Cass."
Here was his woman, the main event,
his feature flick, the star he followed
down the highway that fine cloudless day.

He'd seen her around, they'd talked just once
at a gallery where she worked part-
time but with heart. Among the sad nudes
she had seemed proud, like a cougar clothed
in sandy tan.
                    Almost a month slid
before he saw her again; this time
she said, "Where have you been?" as if she'd
been expecting him, and he disarmed,
told her half the truth, "Avoiding you."

"That's a silly thing to do. Why so?"
"It hurts to look at you."
                              "You say
the nicest things. Does this line ever
work? What are you trying to pick up—
sadists?"

          "You've just explained my first wife…"
"I don't want to hear it—not just now—
let's go somewhere." She scribbled on a card,
"Gone Fishing." And that's what they did.

Sort of. One of the directors of
the gallery, a doctor, oft left
his office in the afternoons just
such a sign upon his own door, but
he really meant it, his love of sport
now dominating his job and life.
Did Cassie, On go fishing or not
for the kind of life they may have caught?

IV. The Poet Flirts with Fame

Onagain's first book of poems, *First Light*,
appeared from Hellebore Press, a press run
of fifteen hundred copies. Last count
he had three hundred and seventy-
three left in some boxes in the front
closet. This, believe it or not, was
no publishing nightmare; a success,
rather, greater than Thoreau and his
seven hundred and six remaining
boxed in his attic. So Onagain
glided among writers' groups, famous
in three cities. They asked him to read
"Shades of Blue" more than once, till, indeed,
he had it by heart: "Aquamarine
scenes / Monterey rays / Cobalt blue-eyed
skies / Paint me? You could, / Straight from the tube."

If he read with rising inflection
where you'd normally let the voice trail
off in the ditch like a bowling ball,
they heaved a collective sigh, when he
stalled like an airplane wing at the end
of the poem. On's next book, *Noon Treasons*,
was accepted for the MacAlbright
competition for the best new book

by an author of one book no less
than thirty years of age and whose verse
defied categories of gender—
which means, not male, nor female, nor queer.

If I've decried most occupations—
the realtors and psychologists,
the prophets of Esalen and Zen
and even poets—it's not because
I think that enemies are useful.
Slander I think as American
as applesauce. You can even win
the presidency with sly insults
as late in the eighties, Horton,
Willie, was portrayed as the best friend—
in fact, closer than Dad or blind date—
of Mike Dukakis, candidate.
Since Horton was a murd'rer, his race
was denigrated; his friend lost face.
Or how the child of John McCain
was Asian, making him Don Juan.

On set a course down supermarket
aisles, avoiding hydrolized proteins,
propyl gallate and the Charbydis
of saturated fats. On between
the Scylla of cholesterol-rich
cheeses and oils. To read these labels
required patience. Nine point four ounces

versus four point nine at just past half
the price. Recently, most things turn out
cheaper the smaller the box he bought.
Shopping improved the mathematic
skills he used to teach the poetic.

But, Reader, these verses are missing
one syllable for pentameter:
This is no way to pentambulate,
always shy one syllable. What walks
on five feet? She asked. Onagain thought,
"You mean, besides Shakespeare's verse?" but tried
not to sound professorially smug,
"You haven't met my cousin." Chuckles
rippled through the class. Non-"P.C."
as the Eightees were, "An amputee
insect? A drunk dragging his nostrils?
An elephant? a triplegic
spider? three-legged dog and his master?
Two crippled men with only one cane?
Assorted limbless gray Arachnids?
Someone doing pushups with his head?
Ask me tomorrow. I really hate
To leave no way to pentambulate."
As I was sitting down to write this,
Cupid was it or some mobster thief
stole a foot, just as two thousand years
ago, almost to the day, the same
thing happened to P. Ovidius
Naso, Ovid to you, that guy we

all liked then. Such a jokester he was.
Got him in trouble, too. Augustus
said he corrupted his daughter's mind.
That'd take some doing. What she has
I'd best not say, but she surely was.

Whatever Augustus said was law,
cast in stone, so when he said, "Away!
To Tomi!"

       That was it for Ovid
and his light airy verses. His *Ars*,
Ovid's Ars, gave advice, how to
pick up women at sports stadiums.

       If she spills crumbs down on her sweater,
          Lightly brush whatever's there,
        Although it's not like crumbs, just brush it...
He'd be arrested now, Ovid would,
as he was back then, come to think...

                      How
I miss him now that poetry's glum,
beat the drum—dum-da-dum—sound profound
and sad, so sad. Ovid even said
he would write profoundly, in epic
verse form, but that mad impulse, "Cupid"
(the Roman word for impulse) that took
his breath away. My last sigh came out
one breath short of pentameter lines.

And I too notice how it's quite hard
to fit American speech into
iambic pentameter, though Frost
did, and Bishop, and some others, too.
Even "AM bic pent AM et er"—it's
more dactyllic, now, won't you admit?

Forgotten Prolog: This Form

Stroke and slide, to the right, to the right
always because this is English, not
Hebrew and to the left. Break even
on the last syllable, or in what
stands in the middle, though there can't be—
What's half of nine? Keep it moving, keep
it up, at a fine pace. Internal
rhyme is possible at caesuras,
as in "nine" and "fine" above except
only David Brinkley would pause, cause
a caesura between "fine" and "pace."
Almost never end at the line end.
Almost always keep there a stressed beat.
Do we repeat acatalectic
pentameter, or does it differ?
Stroke and slide, move and groove; amphibrachs,
like this one, and this one, and this one.

To be a poet is to apply—
not praxis of craft, applications
for jobs. Onagain averaged some
seventy equal opportunity
requests, "Is your speech impaired? Hearing?"
He imagined some heavenly world
where language was unnecessary
for teaching. "Partial paralysis?
Complete paralysis?" Consider
the courage of such a job hunter.
Did this form offer false promises
for such an applicant? Or should he
boast of something wrong, his vision dim
from reading in low light, his speech slurred.
He had always felt slow-witted; had
he the spunk to put it on parade?

Surely those who write *are* handicapped,
stricken with a curse and a burden.
Give writers a special parking place
to ease their stupid career choices.
Why not? Or pay them to stay at home,
out of everybody's way. That might
fix 'em up right, that might do the trick.
And poets! They should be fed by tube,
intravenous, they're so out of it.
Suicides like Sexton, Plath, and John
Berryman; and drunks like Berryman,
Dylan Thomas, almost everyone
writing in the last fifty years. Drunk.

Fame was the compensation. Famous
in three cities, Onagain found girls
liked him better as he aged—lovely
girls, too. He couldn't figure it.
Had he lost that haunted look that young
men carry, that so disfigures them?
In high school the young melancholic
often dressed in a dark blue sweatshirt

and *dungarees*—the Bombay word for *jeans*,
the French for Genoa. Pairs of pants
wander the world on Himalayan
trekkers, on hitchikers in Boston,
seeking their origins. As for me,
I know mine too well, my pedigree.

The Crosley truck carries trash barrels
rattling in back, empty, back when metal
was the only barrel. To a new
house, rooms empty, hardwood floors stretching
to papered wall and fireplace. Lights on
over apartment mailboxes—this
or the truck my earliest memories
(and *Donkey, Donkey* with his bloody
ear, and *The Little Engine that Could*.)

In brittle air the sun sneaks around
crouching on the horizon. Light streaks
through, but clouds bottom blue-black.
The dim drumbeat of a football game
down the hill. But here it's a flat plain
and the rhythmic thunder comes
from a parked car's rock song. The same skies,
the same drum, the same dumb aggression,
but different games.
                              Different seasons—
in May he grew greedy for trees
in flower, the shadbush petals
rain on his wet car, a bridal sprinkle,
wet spectacle. Hold on until when
the beachplum blooms white, or the Scotch broom.

At thirty-one he was sleeping with
the sexiest girl he'd known, which was
a problem. He kept telling himself
she had no ordinary body,

told himself he was a happy man.
Strange, that happiness requires effort,
a greater imagination than
any other, just to imagine
oneself happy. That Mercedes man
needs us watching, wanting. We oblige.
Of course we do, some of us, sometimes;
but that moment of desire pleases
more than possession, especially

owning without imagining us
wanting. This makes ownership forlorn
just as a lover in possession
of her fondest desire may not come
until she dreams how on the sidewalk
one she passed desiring her unknown.
It is from this we suffer in mind,
O my America, O my land
not quite promised. Satisfaction needs
imagination, while Mick Jagger
can't get none. It is from abrasion
of our imaginings we suffer.
Shrinks bill half of us.
                              Polynesia!
Where no child cries—they're never set down.
One supposes such unalloyed joy
leads to satisfied imaginings.
At least Micronesia rewarded
Margaret Mead, but perhaps island
men dream on New York and Hollywood.

O my, my America! Onnie
lost in the land of fatal distraction.
Just you look at the television
on Saturday afternoons, just look
at interminable games like Rome's.

What's this about? A nation of kids.
Do you really think that Disneyworld
sells to children? And dogfood to dogs?
What cash can the dogs and kids release?
I'm preaching now, because On is gone
to the next canto, half of his song.

V. Job Search, Auntie Frieda and the Dog

What're his chances. He needs work, but
jobs were thin. One opened at a home
for the elderly, activities
director. Slumped in their chairs they wait
for the momentous event, at bat
for the last time, their "ups." Would they hit,
get on base? Onagain cheered them on,
he urged them, Prepare for the Big Game.
Were they ready? Who was he fooling?
The game was almost over. They'd lost.
They blew it. How could he keep their minds
from despair.
                    Youth had filled with promise,
a big lead which age had stolen in
one inning. Twenty-one to nothing
when they were young, and now they had lost.
It would be his job to teach them how
to die in bed, on feeding tubes. Now.

First, forget the good times. Think of when
your first girlfriend left with that sneaking bum.
Sisters, consider your kids, the ones
who don't visit. Remember them young,
the snow jacket with mittens tied on
with yarn through the arms. One is dangling
as I tell this, your child is walking

at two years old, towards the kitty
on the neighbors' back stoop. "Bpet kit-ty?"
she says, and your heart breaks for the joy
you could not feel then.
                              Too busy with
the next meal, those pink chapped cheeks, the next
paycheck, the babysitter, her waif's
clothing, in the photo. Poverty,
you had forgotten blessedly what
this evidence documentary
proves clearly. Recall her poverty.

Onagain knew here's the job for him.
Coaching Madame Devereux to meet
her maker, or to forget cancer,
whichever was less painful he'd do.
Turned out, neither was all that easy.
He first joined Mrs. Crumbles' table,
told them they were dining with poets.
Tennyson, dressed all black, what did he
eat but boiled beef and stew of mutton?
Keats hardly ate at all, birdlike, his
nightingale a light consommé,
a soup, a sumptuous feast of sounds.

Poets Dine at Home

Matthew Arnold traveled the world
and knew good meals after he'd eaten

them, as critical intelligence
knows a good baseball game after it's
played, the best novelist when she has
died, a great epoch during the next.
Back in the Renaissance, that's the last
time our poets were great savorers.

Think of Herrick, yes Robert, who wrote
on the merest aroma of meat,
said the gods liked it, though they don't eat.
And the tavern scenes with Shakespeare's Hal
and Falstaff, who ate a bit of bread
to absorb all the sack on his tab.
Of all those blind drunks who wrote poems,
Dylan Thomas comes first to mind,
whose pickled Welsh innocence sold well
for a time; and S.T. Coleridge,
on opium; and the man I rode
the St. Paul bus with, John Berryman,
Gentleman John, who politely thanked
the busdriver everytime he debarked.

The three ladies at table, thank God,
are not listening. One talks like this,

"Sissis- sissis, don't you see, Adelle,
I have to." But there's no Adelle there
(Francine and Lottie at his table).
How fortunate he is not t'have
an hostile audience. Such is life
for the poet—and as for most men,
when they get old, they get all funny.
Poets do not have to wait so long.

Onagain thought he should have brought them
to his last poetry reading when
the college planned a centennial
event. They'd celebrated a fete.
Invited to read, Onagain sat

impressed by the patient audience,
awaited his turn. The second poem
of the second reader started thus,
"His ego bled all over my rug,
My white shag or was it braided?
The stains remain." She rocked portentous,
(inaudible) " ...In Your Shorts!" Applause.
Shouts of "Yes!" "You tell 'em, Babe," murmured
the crowd. Many, like him, had not heard.
Undeterred, she read about her ex,
"In what dank part of you / Should I affix
My red tag, 'Sold!'/ How hide the raw flesh
of my anger?" Again the sharp shriek
of a whistle as to a loose dog.

On she read unflinching as before
the blitzkrieg of memories what dived
ending the poem, her voice subsides
into husk. Pauseless she digresses
on Shell Oil Company (they're raping
manifold lands, those evil men.)
Onagain rose to read after a tall
man, when he felt he had heard it all.

After he had read from *Noon Treasons*,
he read an autobiography,
Poet Onagain's Song, Section One.
A chuckle or two emerged, so he
knew he'd better give up poetry,
he'd be doomed to anthologies of
light verse by the later Robert Frost
and Ogden Nash, maybe Vikram Seth.
Later at the wine and cheese, that Beth
accosted, "Well, Onnie, you still here?"
Did she expect him to disappear?

What could he say. He was at a loss.
Simple exchange made him crapulous.
"Gee, it must be fifteen years!" she said,
to which he managed, "D'ya have a dog?"
Now wait just a freakin' minute, here—
what the hell are you doin', Onnie,
reading my poem. It's just not fair,
since you're engaging, shy, and funny,

and I don't exist 'cept on a page,
that you just steal it. I'm in a rage!
It's not your autobiography!
It's a Byronic satire, you bum,
you sexist, self-indulgent, lazy
bastard. You just write pab'lum, snot.
You keep this up and I will commit
suicide, not you—then where'd you be?
Lambasting, I was fried when Frieda,

"Now you leave my Onnie, lay off your
threats. Kill yourself! No big likelihood
of that. The people that really should
never commit. You should be ashamed.
Onnie has a right to use what you
Misrepresent," she said. "It's his life
you depend on. You non-Romantics
feed on others' lives, like my genius
nephew. My brother never treated
that kid right, thought he should do more chores,
take the trash out, help his drunken dad
to clean up where he dropped the bottle.
Onnie's life at home was plain awful."

After Auntie was done with me, I
remembered Beth had no dog. So On's
puppy Wordsworth mumbled to himself.

A Dog's Tale

Of many words I have no need,
   Like all those human lies—
Say, where they've been. With one stiff sniff
   I know, the noser knows.

I'm no sapiens, I'm canine.
   I drop my nose down on
A pile of leaves and some coins,
   Move on barely pawsing.

Hard money smells, but not enough.
   I root out putrid pods
In leaves Boreas left, then bark
   At fiend Boreas' moan

Through yellow trees and toasted oaks
   This brisk October dusk.
I truffle by the mailbox post
   To piss—oops—missed the pole

But hitting my front leg. What whiffs
   By the pond, what long sniffs,
The residue of stag and duck,
   Heron and otter, murky frog.
In a cowpatty field I lie
   Scentient of rabbit or muskrat,
My nose up to the breeze.
   Sometimes I tug like a vacuum

On roadside rug, this way, that
   I follow twisting isobars
Of scent, map resident
   Traffic patterns, confluent trails.

That rat-tailed possum
   And pink-pawed raccoon both end,
Their last stand. My lowered head
   Shows I'm worried, too, about
How mortality stinks.
   But at least my nose tells no lies.
I nose enough, I thinks.

Wordsworth, a reflective poet pup,
wrote the above while sniffing some posts
for a mile. Was it rhyme doggerel?
Leave it to fangy critics to tell.

Auntie Frieda, fierce defender, chose
her hearted causes, niece or nephew,
fought for them in total war, her frame
so stolid belying her nervous heart.

Built like Gertrude Stein, with curly hair,
her Ohio vowels sounded more
assured than she was. Her secret vice,
a five year correspondence with nice
male strippers, the Chippendales. Good boys,
though naughty, she would not hear them called
gay, and she said so in her letter
to Rosie O'Donnell, whose answer
she prized, planning a plain lacquered frame.

Frieda worried sick about Laura,
whether she would stay with Luke
after they were married. In Monday mood
she'd watch most anything, kids on trikes
knocked down by the pet dog, HA; kneeling
grey-haired lady falls into a bush,
rises, staggers; the man bicycling,
waving at the camera, jolted
by a rut into the grass. Funny,
funniest home videos, they said.
Yes, but Frieda only half believed.

Auntie taught typing and dictation,
knew her students by where they had sat,
like third from the windows way in back,
in three-oh-one. But once dictations
started, she kept on despite pigeons
screwing on the quoins. She still kept on
through sonic booms, even a fire drill

(those huge old windows sure did rattle)—
on through sirens and some pistol shots,
through four changes in department heads:
> On through Nixon's resignation,
> On and on she gave dictation,
> On past Watergate, through Carter,
> On when students begged for water,
> On throughout the hostage crises,
> On through Onagain's devises.

Years later she retired to a huge
new place with hundreds of residents,
but needed canes to get to dinner.
Though she still kept her car, her humor,
Frieda was too much for the nurses,
who invited a psychologist,
noting this: "Frieda Max presented
as a heavy, neatly-dressed grey-haired
woman who looked younger than most all
the residents. Her hypomanic
affect masks an angry mood, how we
were stupid, trying to fool her but
we don't, especially not that guy
writing the long poem about her
nephew Onnie. Clutter, piles of mail
grow in corners of her studio
apartment. I diagnose grapho-
philia, the love of written words
(she refuses to toss printed ones),
on top of bipolar disorder.

"Though on the Folstein Mini-Mental
she got twenty-nine out of thirty,
I urge that she be tested further
to rule out bipolarity—and
rule out any disease we can treat,
and too, check on her ataxic gait."

Dr. Liz never stumbled upon
Frieda's letters to the Chippendale's,
which would have changed her diagnosis
from problems as ataxic walker
to possibly a female stalker.
We know her as less harmful than,
say, her brother and his obsession.

VI. The Campus Sky

A vast expanse of moody sea, when
      the spirit opens out, released, Onagain
      at night confronted, as it turned out
      Orion in Spring, Scorpio now.
As when racing across a barren
wall of night, punctuated by five
of the brightest stars, Orion's belt
and fuzzy sword, nebula, Rigel,
Procyon, Betelgeuse, Sirius,
the night train hesitates and slows
at an old iron canopy. Look!
A vast city rises, sprinkles lights
like a stadium constellation.
Onagain looked for labels, for some
name. Syracuse, with its Greek theater?
Rochester its Polaroid boardroom.

No vistas, no prime realty could he claim
(What are all those spectator houses
lining the bay's edge waiting for, what
celebrity will wash in on
the dawn tide?) No prime realty,
but on a gray day, the trees leafing
like dieters, less full, like adolescence
promise-laden, hopeful but sparse,
he can leave the distractions of sight,

the hustle of mind, the noisy
visions, and hear twitters, chirrups, rasps,
and rasping tweets, all the eloquence
of pitch and pause. He strains to focus
on the grousy warning fricatives
pierced by piping—Weegee gee Keek,
keck, keck. Keckeck. Weegeegee Keek.

Birds talk business, Titmouses' "My Tree!
Get outta my tree!" Territory
they guard, generals of wild cherry,
corporals of oak. These guys have guts,
they'll grapple as grackles with a hawk,
all day, not just in wartime. They live
in a war zone, all of 'em. Robins
had built in a small spruce, and fended
off jays every day. Jays like fresh eggs,
but took to eating dogfood. Onnie
sympathized with the jay's low esteem
of self and low diet, low protein.

The night grove fills with spirits, scratching
in the leaves, a heavy hiss, the spiral
loopey Screech owl, so-called, so small
you never see them, but you hear 'em,
and they terrify the Mourning Doves.
And say truth: walk in the moonless dark
at the edge of the wood, coyotes
near enough to hear you breathe. Terror?

Horned Owls, silent as grass, or as Swans,
which they kill with just one red, deep peck
in the back of their neck.
                                        Why do they slice
what they won't eat? For fun—or for practice.

So night fills in the Fall, migratory
midnights off the Carolina coast
Onnie at sea saw coming on deck
Scorpios rising, the stars and he.
Do the birds take starry bearings? No,
more likely they follow the coast down,
watch the black sea gleam in the moonlight,
see the beacon lights and lighthouses,
try hard to miss the hum, the windfarms
springing up like swamp grass and its plumes.

Someone should clean up the heavens, they're
really a mess. You can never find
what you left there a week or two past.
Tonight he was lost to find so huge
Pegasus just where he'd left it, next
to that dither of Aquarius
so indistinct but highly touted.
And the whole closet had been moved
to the other end of the house. True,
last time he'd looked this time a night was
weeks ago, before the cloudy nights.
Here in New England there's always that

to keep the surprise. Then when he'd looked
for it, Pegasus was on the front lawn
and something brave—oh, Scorpio—
by the crabapple out back. That's changed,
and now it's moonless, it's more silent.

Onnie'd heard Carl Sagan say "Beelions
and beelions" of what? Not stars, not earths,
but whole galaxies. Vast whirling wastes,
where somewhere, Giordano Bruno states,
another world, another hundred
thousand worlds contend for attention
from Saviors and leaders of all stripes.
In a Roman Prison, the Tor di Nona,
he begged paper to answer the charge,
and Aquinas to footnote his brief,
and at age fifty-one, for the first
time, eyeglasses.
Bruno's mistake, not to see that his
universe—or his "turner-as-one"—
turned Christ into Santa, saving here,
saving there, on another planet.
Nope, Pope wouldn't hear a word of it.

No one wants to hear of other worlds
that don't include us. Giordano
knew Ficino by heart, gravity
of Love holding Venus and the Earth,
their solar circumrevolutions,

as surely as Love embraces babies
and long-haired dogs. Will love last until
we encounter one from beelions,
one world out there with creatures unlike
any we know yet? Or will we fry
long before we catch their radio waves ,
their music like birdsong without staves.

Colleges buzzed with culture, no not
opera and dance, that sort of thing,
but different foods and speech, like collard
greens and Southern dialect, Boston
brahmin and vegetable tempura.
Part-time Onagain talked punishments
cruel and unusual. Teens liked
to discuss the gruesome, and Onnie
didn't mind. What about beheading?
"That was reserved for the aristocrats,
the Earl of Essex, rich clientele..."
Sheila cooed, "Yech."
                              "Because it's faster
than hanging, which can last several hours.
'Course there's an art to execution,
called it a 'mystery' or a profession."
"Some profession," Travis offered from
the back row, "What guild accepted them?"
Onnie didn't know—not farriers,
not fletchers, dyers nor cutlers— "None.
You know the guillotine's invented
by a French physician, Guillotin

in order to make execution more humane.
But the guillotine just sped it up,
the first machine of revolution—
the Industrial one, which built mills
to busy those Marie Antoinette
had taunted, "Let them eat cake."
Travis kept on pondering the guild,
the Barber-Surgeons made him feel ill.

Onnie noticed his students perked up
to brutality. Raised on T.V.,
they watched what he avoided. Horror
shows, blood spurting from eyeball sockets,
he felt blinded. Every murder killed
something in him, but it seemed to feed
the kids. He said, "You know their baseball,
their national sport was bear-baiting.
Down the street from Shakespeare's Globe Theatre
stood the Bear-Bayting Ring."
                              "How'd that work?"
Todd asked. "Well, they'd bet on the dogs,
then sick them at the bear; he'd get bit
around his ear or rear, blood would drip." Sheila almost
yelped, "Aiii can't see that.
Now, if their culture was used to it,
you know, the executions, they can
accept it. But hurting dogs, that's sick."
On smiled at her, so species correct.

After class, at his office he found
Eddy who'd enrolled in Creative
Writing, "My tuition will be paid
by a state vocational grant. News,
you know, is mostly one's tone of voice."

"That so? How's your course going?"
                                        "My prof
says we should give up all our personal
references. But they add irony,
don't they? I know every cop within
twenty miles, all quite different, some friends,
like Antone. I guess she's afraid we'll
reveal drug deals, leave her culpable.

 "Well, nice to see ya. I'm off to a
battery of tests, my third."
                                "Your third?"
"Yes, I've had the Minnesota Multiphasic
for vocational advisement, some
intelligence test with blocks, circles
and cones. Now this one's to make sure
I'm stable enough to cope with school,
what with life in my Buick and all."
"I thought all exams check on that—mine
do, for sure.   Keep cool, and you'll do fine."

Sitting in McDonald's one bright May,
On stares through the near heat on brown grass,
the carsplash pools and puddles, the slow
painful sunlight, stares out the
fishbowl glass at the silvery fishcars
swimming silent, finning their way
in the stream of light—when from
another booth, the sound of teenage
boys, "Look at that guy. D'ya suppose
he's got all his marbles?" "Seems to me
he's got a screw loose. Weird, man, out there
like off the freakin' wall."

       He said, and raised
a french-fry toward the hole in his head.

Saved! His colleague Armand joined him
deep in an exchange with humble Tim,
"I think that's a very important
point Armand's making. Tell Onnie here,"
"Sure. I want to decreate this to
a psychopoetic level, say
Mallarme's take, how he relates to
female sexuality. It seems
he's doing a sort of Jungian-
Olsenian schtick without Olsen's
aleatory found-logic gestalt."

"Sirs, what'll you have to drink?"
"Coffee for me." "Make that another."

"Isn't it interesting, really,
that Mallarme uses the masc'line
form of 'le' when he had no choice?"
                                        "Hnn?
Obviously, the grammar calls for the
masculine." "But that's just my point. If
the grammar calls for it, why doesn't
he do the opposite, like cummings."

On the Road to Mallarmé,
Let us dance the night away.

"I didn't order orange soda."
"No, well who did then, who did?"
"What's it to me? I told you, not me.
I'd never order chocolate, either;
Chocolate's a bourgeoise distraction—
it's to keep them from revolution."
"Well, then, may I ask what you ordered?"
"I haven't ordered yet, that's the point."
"What would you like?"
                                "That orange soda
looked good as you were dumping it out."
"But you refused one."
                                "It wasn't mine."
"I won't waste another, they'll fire me."
"It won't be wasted."
                                "I can't chance it."

"You're refusing to serve me?"

"Yes, sir."

"What if I order a chocolate,
like the one you're holding?"

"Here, take it."

"I don't want it, I didn't order,
I just asked what if I did. No-one
understands subjunctive anymore."
"Are you trying to get on my nerves?"
"What if you deliver something that
the person didn't order?"

"What if?"

"Could I then get that order for none?"
"Yes, but what if it's an orange drink."
"I wouldn't order orange soda."

Editor's Preface

This is a modern poem, whose hero
you will meet, though you may not notice
any features to distinguish him
from an Ordinary Joe or Jo.
The period of which we speak—
neither punctuational, still less
menstrual, but demi-rhetorical-
histor'cal—as anyone can see
in such an era one lacks terms
with which to filigree. A whatnot
of a Time to live at. The very
most etcetera I ever saw.
Well, you know yourself
how nations juggle several wars
at once, killing just enough voters
to make the rest damn glad to prosper
within their sealed-up borders. Yes, and
I can be precise: Greek and Turk

fight over Troy and Cyprus, Arab
and Jew kill each other in the street
of Jericho or Sidon, West and East
misjudge each other, misunderstand.
Historically, we can place the year
sometime within the last four thousand.
Time, they say, passes, while we, yes, flunk.

Textual Note

The poet appears to have left the
following fragments in haste, mere
traces of a body of thought which
were we to know its entirety
might prove unintriguing. But as they
stand now, broken, suggestive, they
rise almost as the warm vapor over
frosty leaves where in winter Words-
worth pissed.

                These breathy intimations
of thought are timeless in two senses:
yes, there is no secure dating of
their origin, nor even complete
agreement on the culture from which
they rose: was it in fact the hoe
culture of the mesolithic period, or more
properly viewed as the bronze age mystical
cult known familiarly as the "smokers"
for their preference for burning
damp wood. They preferred smoke to fire,
as somehow more approachable, more degagée.

These fragments remain, as Port Royal
said of Pascal, an unfinished temple—
exuding vapors, pious, intimate.

VII. Sexidermy

Home after two classes at two schools.
Cassie had moved in two weeks ago.
In her other job, Cassie combined
aromatherapy and Tai-Chi
to combat low back pain. She'd studied
biofeedback, Tai Chi Ch'uan Yang style,
and Aikikado, but no black belt
for her. She couldn't summon the force
and speed to anticipate, though
she dreamed of Aikikado practice.

Army basic would not be amiss.
Not Reggae, but Rekei therapy
like seventies Bioenergy.

"You've got to check these mats for ticks,"
Onnie's Dad said petting Wordsworth,
who heard uneasy verse in his head.

A Dog's Appendage

And another thing, are you
  Listening to me?
I smell a rat. You humans do
  Keep us caged up, see.

We were here long before Native
  Americans, and now
You tie and bind us. See if
  I come when you bow-wow.

What are my opportunites?
  My breed should have stayed
In Asia with the Samoyed
  Tribe. There we were payed.
Some valued us higher than wives,
  And why not? Our love doesn't fade.

The dog seemed in a trance of thought
while the Dad waxed plain avuncular,
 "But I just don't understand you young
guys. You know I have those apartments
for rent?   It's always the girls, that's who,
they're the ones who come and rent. The guys
show up, move in later. Sit at home
and let the woman work. I just don't
understand it."
                "Not us. I'm a chip
off the old block."
                "Now if you ask me
women have had the power always,
the control of men. You agree, Cass?"

"No. All better paying jobs at banks
are men's. They don't tell you when they hire.

Instead, they say something like, you'll get
performance reviews ev'ry three months.
They don't say, 'And if you're dating me
by then, you're all set. No, they rather
you found that out later…"

                                    "Now, just you
wait a minute, hold on, you're broadly
stereotyping now."

                        "And you're not?"
"I'm talkin' real life, the kind I saw
in the service. Tell me how in hell
is a dame gonna piss over rail
on midnight watch? Naw, she'll go and use
the head, 'I've got to powder my nose.'

"And how are the guys gonna do it
now either, with her watchin? It don't
make sense, that's all. Plain as a baby's ass,
or the lady's, either, hung over
the rail—can't you see it now? Moonlit."

"You need some Ginseng root
or something. You just wish you'd been there.
When I have clients your age, I urge
them to try aromatherapy
or just a little bit of Tai Chi."

Cassie knew him better than she knew,
though she had never seen the jeweller's
vice on which he tied flies from feathers
he collected—Wood Duck, Osprey,
Canada Goose, Hermit Thrush, Card'nal,
Pine Siskin—or Badger hair sent for
from catalogs. His flies were beauties,
shimmery. At first he fished with them
in adolescence, until he found
out mermaids, with their mothlike tails
yet fishy, too. They were rare species,
his girls, samples and varieties.

Bucktail he needed to make Muddlers
(Whitlock or Searcy's). For Marabou
he found the underdown of Heron
did just fine. For tied fly heads, bucktail
not calves'. He would not buy baby seal
fur to make Atherton's Light Nymph, though
badger and Golden Pheasant he bought.
The hackles of the Guinea Hen? Bright
white and black fly wings. Blue Herons cry
like a rusty door; Golden Pheasants,
like a rusty car but more in pain.
Fiery brown glints golden turned to sun.

This was what began his tail collection:
flyfishing turned to dating, the same
fuzzy texture of the muff and breast
of Robin, the same lowtide odors.
His habit of collecting, to pick
up the hair or feather that you see;
it seemed a natural transition.

So now he kept in his gun chest, locked
lockets of his girls' nether eyebrows.
Trophies, yes. Bristly blond pubic hairs
would make an ideal Silver Nymph,
knotted next to curly fine brown wires
from Cecelia's seat of her desires.

His box of boxes held no beaver
fur, though as beavery as could be;
there lay innocent ringlets of hair,
one the hue of red squirrel, and some
the color of the thrush. One appeared
to be a horse's mane, bristley; weird,
how natural dad's collection looked
until you considered. He had fucked
these women and kept telltales, witness
testimonials, like fishing lures
and mole fur, or bouncing rabbit tails.

Onnie's never seen this cigar box,
didn't know his dad beyond what he
could stand. Nor would his father ever
confess his obsession, though he had
shown two buddies, fishermen ten years
since. Sometimes he feared that they might
send the police. Or if something happened
to one of his former girlfriends, and
his name came up. Onnie's mom had died,
her hair was there. Dad could see headlines,
"Hairs of Twelve Women Identified"
or worse, "Sexidermist Arrested."

Do we want to know all this, Dad's life?
In middle years, he told his son's wife,
"The sirens—everytime I hear I
think of fourth floor at the orphanage
'cause we were shown all you know those reels
newsreels with the Germans bombing us,
all I could think of. And we'd be asked
to pray for the Pope. He could do no
wrong. In-fall-i-ble. He pooped icecream.
My mother'd left me there, dressed me in
a black suit and took me to those nuns.
I'm scared of these three sisters—big smiles—
but they look weird. And to a kid—well,
I thought if I leave she'll leave and I'll
never see her again. Me having
to go to the bathroom but I don't.
"I try to hold on till she goes, Ma.

I wet 'em walking that long corridor,
thinking, Where's Tippy? Where's Tammy? Ma?
When I walk into this room where
all the kids are sitting at a long
table. Eating supper, oatmeal. One
kid right next ta me, he didn't want
the stuff, refused. She took his head, pushed
it right into the bowl, that nun.
Right then I said, Hold on, I better get
a grip on this, I've got to watch it.

"—The smell of people! The dirt, even!
So nice! 'Cause all that was was wood floors.
We walked in twos. You know the worst thing
they could do to me? Just stand me and leave
me in a corner of the hall. I'm
thinking, Will they ever come back?
We couldn't none of us talk to girls,
my sister, even. O yes, she was
there, too, for eight years, eight. Never spoke.
Couldn't even look at the girls, No.
Not even your own sister. But I
saw her through the fence sometimes, recess.
And I was molested by a nun...."

VIII. Parodies, Paradose

Dad had left when Cassie admitted
she had a third job, one that sure made
Onnie agitated. "You should quit
that." "Why?"

                 "You know why." "No, I do not."
"Because I don't want everybody
and his brother staring at you nude."
"Mostly it's everybody's sister.
Don't you enjoy Venus di Milo,
       Ingres' Odalisque? You told me so."

"I wasn't planning to live with them."
"That's so possessive, so bourgeoise."

                          "Hmm."

True, Onnie liked possession of her
and of styles, he thought to imitate
verses by our poet laureate,
but which one? Wasn't Ben Jonson first,
and his deft disciple Bob Herrick,
his lyrics atmospheric. On tried,

    "Give me a watch when I retire
        To tell the time I need not know;
    Give me a camera now I'm fat
        To take the picture I'd rather not;

Give me champagne when I'm fired,
        Give me coffee when I'm tired:
And I will give to you
A Christmas present, too.

I'll give you perfume to entrance
        Nostrils—that are made in France;
I'll give you nightgowns to allure
        The milkman, and the carpenter;

I'll give you jewelry to confer
        To rival—or to pawnbroker:
And you will know that I
Love you to the sky."

He felt he'd caught it, just a bit, that
sev'nteenth-century ironic wit,
then turned to the one American
whose genius had also captured it.

He didn't plan to, but he did spend
a year on Emily Dickinson,
her birds, her pets, until he mastered,

        "I practice Dying—every night—
            But have not learned to, still,
        Though Talented—by mortal Bones—
            For such a Common Skill."

But that's the easy part, genius
much the easier to copy than
our quotidians. Just allow *Vox*,
as Shakespeare's Feste says.   Who's up next?
There's all those Sensitives, those who write
polemics like On's fellow poets
chasing fame. Besides hapless husbands,
the Holocaust, the Middle Passage,
there's the Blowjob lyric, a genre
now in the Twenty-First Century—
one could trace it from Ginsberg on to…
but let's not. There's the Hospital Ode
and then, Environmental Epode.

There was that wild Welshman, Dylan, drunk
on America, the college tour
singing,
        "Love-burst firth, froth on the sea
Foams on the surf. Life burst first from the
edge of the sea, leapt spume over land,

arched sparkling, fell seed into soil
to the rhythm of crests. Swollen sounds
drown the gulls' song. Crying, the waters
rode the coast down. Hour by hour,
the granite shelf wore to endure
the ponderous surge of interm'nable
urge, and ebb."
        He read in his mellow
tenor, tuning around middle C.

The other Dylan had no voice, bawled
out his own rainy day songs, like,

                      "Slide

into love," a toboggan of weed
growing roadside in Minnesota
missed by National Guard flame-throwers,
"We never did too much walkin' anyway."
Lake Woe-ful harmonica wailing.

Closely allied to nature pieces
Creeley warned us of dead pets, a sub-
genre of the elegy, but is
it the love elegy or true one?
The beauty of the paws a raccoon
exhibits unwilling, struck in the road—
which Bill Stafford the definitive
wrote of the deer we all have read,
seen a hundred times on I-80.
Tiny Dickinson treated all birds
as reluctant pets, so Onnie tried,

      "You know she did not have her choice
          Because she doesn't run.
      She never trusted anyone
          Least of all the One

      Who lowers her resistless down
          And still repeats a name.

      Save for her eyes, as grey as Dust—
          As gray as dust to dust.

Her wide gold eyes have widened
In that Surprise, her last."

Onnie could go on like this, but when
Would he sound contemporary-rare?
Better to begin with modern styles,
something in a sporty look perhaps,
something jaunty, uncapitalized,
asyntactic at the least, the best.
For this, he knew just the voice, urbane
With insouciance, juicy and wasted,
not to be believed, a street-wise guy,
the Voice of the Village. He tried this,

"Had you noticed the primavera
as you came through the loggia? Go
back and look I say, seated. Many
have missed the cotillion. But I wish
them well from the alley or first floor.
It is never too late for the opera.
It is always too late for the Big Bang."

His verse grew vast, urban, Ash-buried,
soot-footed, exhaustive and converted,
catalytic more than catalectic,
more cataclysmic, cacaphonic.

Once, like those old Romantics, Shelley,
Keats and Wordsworth, he copied Shakespeare,

> "So I take up my happy pen and turn
>   To truisms and truths about old Time,
> His urgent turnings and his scant returns;
>   I think to make it right with ink and rime.
> If sunsets are like ends, noons are but means;
>   If fires are hot, yet more intense is coal:
> These tired comparisons take up two lines,
>   While you are left to make them true and whole."

But all was futile, for those voices
from the past spoke of other peoples,
other scenes. The clatter of horses'
hooves on the dirt, the chatter of men
speaking clipped Yankee— what Onnie needs
is a woman's voice: the downtrodden,
the Wif of Bath proclaiming Abuse!
in marriage, but: the Whip was hers.

Now our dominatrices with whips
are often poets like one from whom
Onnie imitates "Mayan Echoes":

> "You can grind me up like Brewer's yeast
>   And stuff me full of lies.
> You can bake me in a lump of dough,
>   And still like bread I rise.

You can fee me thirty thousand bucks
        Or maybe thirty-five;
You can poison my Muscovy ducks
        But somehow I'll survive.

You can meet me with a limousine
        That has seen better years
You can seat me near Sadam Hussein
        And still I have no fears.

You can say the whore of Babylon
        Wrote poetry like mine.
You can snicker, glouk and cackle on—
        And still I'll be jus' fine.

Does my windiness repulse you, sir?
        Does my chutzpah surprise?
You can beat me like a bolster
        And still, like down, I rise.

I am the book of history
        That you hide on your shelf,
I tell of black captivity
        And captivate myself.

You can offer me more money
        Than plantations ever had,
But I won't take it, honey—
        Or maybe, just a tad.

You may think that I do nothing
        To deserve so high a fee,
But poetry ain't nothing
        Even if it's made by me.

Is elocution nothing? No.
        Is capitalizing Hope?
Is speaking with machismo
        As if I were the Pope?

Besides, I can enunciate
        Clearer than a fart—
Hard words, like "syphilliticate."
        Who says I have no art?

I'll rhyme you till the end of time,
        I'll tire you from the stage.
I'll shame you from your ofay rhyme,
        I'll hound you in old age.

I'm heir to Billie Holiday
        And sister of the true one;
I sing to sing my blues away,
        But more like Rod McKuen."

When Cassie returned and Onnie read
his "Mayan Echoes," she was pissed, "Yes,
yes, you would, wouldn't you?"

                        "What? Would what?"

"Make fun, merciless fun, of others'
adversity."
                    "You don't understand
how parody works."

                    "No? Maybe *you*
don't understand. Look, I'll tell you this.
I'm not sleeping with you tonight."
                                        "Oh,"

and he added to himself, "It's wet
me through, this loneliness."

Alone, he writes, like the Lone Eagle
Or Wilbur and Orville—he wrights
Well-burred, willing himself well birded,

    Mind puts a thought in play like a bat
    Of Mickey Mantle—often grounding out
    But more often popping up some tall hit
    Hanging on the light poles or a low cloud.

    That ball of thought may seven seconds float
    Like gravity's reversal, then may fall
    Decisive and unchallenged and remote
    By Yankee Stadium's centerfield pole.

    It is no longer Thought, but a Home Run
    Or a long out or a routine fly ball—
    But while it was a simile, it came down
    Without a thud, with no noise at all.

Maybe there's better ways to depart
this earth, an epitaph like Scarron's
or Sergei Yesenin, dying young:

> See ya later, my friend, I'll see ya
> My dear one, you're still with me.
> This parting that had to be,
> It promises, I'll see ya.

> Good-bye, my friend, without hand
> Or word. Don't sulk, don't knit brow
> In life, dying's no innovation,
> Nor, for that matter, long life now.

Boredom, *skuchno* the Russian scourge, while
Scarron the French wit left with a flair.

> Who now lies here below
> Did more to pity than envy,
> Endured a thousand deaths
> Before he left this life.

> Pass by, don't make a sound
> And see you don't awake him,
> 'Cause this night is the first
> That poor Scarron lay— sleeping.

A boast from the grave! That was the Age
of Moliere and the Sun King, long past
those Romans like Persius, who died young,
under thirty. Onnie never liked

his rough satires, though intentional.
But I find in him a young Pushkin;
a bit like this his prolog went:

> Not along the lonely beaches, nor
> From scenery and mountain views, do I
> Remember brooding to become a writer.
> The beaches and the lonely looks, I leave
> To pictures on the backs of books.
> (Myself, I didn't take Creative Writing.)
> Where'd the parrot learn, "Polly wanna
> Cracker," or crows to speak the English?
> From that Master of Arts, Instructor
> Stomach, expressing the inexpressible.
> If there's the faintest hope of copping fame,
> Crowing poets and classroom mavins—
> You'd think we sang like wild hill warblers.

Don't tell me Onagain's Song dates
from Persius, dead at twenty-eight?
Onnie translated him, but forbid Cass
from looking at what he'd done, "It's too crass."

Yet Onnie loved another Roman
who died by thirty, Gaius Catullus.
Young, he traveled to his brother's grave
and wrote immortal, "Salv atque vale,"
> Excuse my useless tears. Brother, so—
> "Goodbye" I greet you, who elude Hello.

All gone, all the young poets: Shelley,
Keats, Arthur Clough, Milton's Lycidas,
Milton whose Paradise was not Lost.
Best not to know too much of the past.

So we leave Onnie in homey bliss,
unaware his Dad's perverted
and that Aunt Frieda writes to strippers
while night cops hassle homeless Eddy
who's the only one with talent
besides the dog and maybe the hag
who writes so fiercely about her ex.
Onnie's making progress—as a chef,
he's on to *gnocchi gorgonzola*
and *spinach with mushrooms and garlic*—
hasn't read a self-help book in years,
but bought a dictionary of half-rhymes
with which he writes these last four lines.
"Better a beetle in a pile of dung
Than anything in a rapper's song."

IX. Rhymes and Echoes

Cut a few years forward, Aura's born
by natural childbirth, that features
Cassie's pain, which On couldn't stand.
He could hear another mother scream
three doors down the corridor, primal
and fearful. There's natural, and more
natural. And then there's Demarol.
Cassie faced it bravely, but couldn't
stay in bed, had to squat for comfort.
He felt his help with a cool washcloth
almost equalled Chopin, the CD
inadequate, after all, to pain.
When she was dilated, they push
her into the birthing room, he smiles,
Doctor Slapp, rubicund. It's a girl.

As foam can fill a bucket, or glass
of draft beer, just so can joy or fear
a nation; a baby fills a house.
Add all the plastic equipages,
supplies, impedimenta in the field
of child-rearing, the pitched battles of
the changing-table, pampers and crib,
the nipples and bottle, or the teat
potable and portable—that's not
to mention the towels and clothes that
fill playpen and bed and bassinette.

Let Cassie and Onnie and Aura
alone in their first year. Let it turn,
the World its annual revolution.
Let the seasons flit, without a bit

of artful regret. Let it go, let
it go, let it go, as the old globe
flies through space, as the constellations
form anew when we look each winter,
each spring. And leave off the jaunty tone
we've told this in, and let that too turn
to tragic. Somehow, we just never learn.

One Saturday snow was forecasted
and it dropped light and windless. Black ice
skinned the pond for the third day, magic
in waiting. By tomorrow you would
have to shovel, the milk ice cloudy.
And Monday, back to classes at noon.
Now's the time. Find the skates he'd sharpened
in March, upstairs in the back closet
to prevent mould.
                              Cassie turned as he
came back down, "Wait, you can take Aura."

Sandy-haired, his curly daughter sat
and puttered on the doghaired rug. What
Wordsworth shed she ate, stuck to her fist
electrostatic. "Want to go out?"

She raised her arms in answer, Pick up
me. He, obedient to gravity,
the force of love, lifted her snowsuit
and her with it, slipped her sideways, zipped
the circuitous lip of the coat.
Ingenuity of children's clothes!
He found his own drab, hooded jacket,
opened the fatal door, and went out.

Wordsworth snuck out too, unimpeded
by Onnie's leg meant to block his way.
Oh what the hey. Why not let him bark
at the new flakes—as he did, pointed
his chin up at the mysterious
manna, while Aura wrinkled her face
to the snowy spice. "Feel funny?" He wiped
her brow with his wrist.

                              She said, "Hot. Hot."
"No, it's cold. Snow is cold." Now wrinkling
just above her nose, she said, "Hot. Hot?"

They walked down the dirt drive, on the paved
road a hundred yards, off on the path
to the pond's verge, dragging the old sled
which grated like metal chalk on stone
blackboard, then sand. Wordsworth shot ahead
onto the ice a pace, slipped, scrambled.
Aura laughed, "Goggie."

                              "Funny doggy,"

Onnie sat on the sled beside her
as he took his boots off, pulled up thick
wool socks and jammed into the black skates.
Wordsworth licked the snow from Aura's blue
snowsuit. It confused some strangers when
they saw the child in blue, with ringlets
curling over her brow. Onnie stood
balanced on the tippy blades, yanked the sled
a foot onto the ice as he stepped
over an air pocket. Wordsworth barked.

The ice spread wide as a plowed black field
in Iowa, black as a painted wall
in Roman Pompei that mirrors light,
a skin above the abyss. Yes, this
is the sublime I study, Onnie thought.
The ice let a deep pop from the end
by the state road. Again Wordsworth barked
from the shore, a Sheepdog, English, slides

sideways, nimble on land. But not ice,
not today. Onnie tugged the old rope
building some speed to swing out Aura
then pull in like a whip. She giggled.

He looked up, saw they were opposite
their cottage, right where he'd always swim
in season. Turning into the wind

from the northwest, he saw darker clouds
and Aura rocking on the sled, "'Gain."
Swinging out then heading back to shore
the sled rope yanked, split. It slid just
ten feet out, then tilted, an icy air
pocket. Aura slipped off, and right there
broke the surface of ice. On tried to rush
toward her, still sliding away, "I'm
COMING!" he shouted, then "HELP! HELP!"
Across the lake it echoed his yell.

His chest constricted as in the dim
light her face crinkled in question. He
reached her as the ice gave way beneath
him and he too fell into the hot
pit, this this abyss, globe below, vast
south pole up, north in the hole of space
below, to my back turning back to
my turn, I hold, hold the will to steer
past night sirens (Where is Arcturus?)
Where oh where has my little Pum gone,
little blond one, my daughter
no, Aura, no Cassie no Father
no one.
          Blackout fell himself between
and his own home, portcullis iron,
but too late, the enemy within.
Reader, I can tell you even weeks
later, as I drove by this Echo Lake
I felt a terror nearby, that stalks

strangers, is it the Death Spirit walks
in that place since native peoples faced
it— whatever the Echo erased
with English. This deep presence sliced
through my driver training, I felt pulled,
my car forced off the roadway toward
the fatal waters. I did not fall
in within down I did not fall in.

But I can see the hot ice, darkly
surrounded by the Shore of Life,
and I hear in the distance Wordsworth
barking frantic on the verge of joy
and sorrow, in between the lost
and the losing, Cassie still waiting
still at home which was now gone that she
didn't know she had lost. As she stood
by a bookshelf where Ficino sat,
in the distance she heard their dog bark
and bark. He had only barked like that
once when a bear appeared at the far
end of the field.
                        His voice scratched
her like a claw, like fear of the sheets
she would see, plastic then linen, white
echoing dark, two lost by the lake,
down the hole in time, Love's gravity
pulled and pulling toward empty space.

Oh where have we arrived with our pen
in the midst of this terrible scene
so far from my intention. Byron

is my hero, Pushkin my model,
but neither seems to have told this tale,
nor certainly, with these characters
so feeble though attractive, somewhat.
Cassie, Onnie, Aura, Frieda, it
seems that they should have fared much better
than Onnie's Dad—or the other poets
like the recent divorcée called Beth.
Or even me, the cumbersome one
scrambling, concocting this abysmal
end: why couldn't they leave hand in hand
through Eden, or build their legacy
in Derby, or marry brothers and
attend a grand event like the real
Onegin, not some thin and surreal
imitation—who's more like Lensky,
anyways. We here on the sidelines
have seen the best plays end in a rhyme,
a jig and a song. It's almost time.

I cannot say how sorry I am
for us both that this is the way it turned
out since together we've had our fun,
even with walk-on parts like Eddy,
Travis and Sheila, Armand and Tim,

Tammy, Wordsworth and Tippy canine,
not to mention Miss Paris and the nun.
I never thought my Onagain, so fake,
so derivative, that he would take
over this vast and chancey scrapbook.
Even when these others seem trivial
hardly human, or, true, demented.
Meanwhile, I do not shrink from the claim
these people have evolved quite beyond
many of their siblings in our lit
and our sad cinema, simpletons
and bullies, wastrels, Americans.

Our novels lack Cervantes' wit
our poems are still Romantic, about
the poets themselves—but do we care
about such grievances, such rare
beasts, such hypoallergenic,
elevated sensitivities.
Give us Cassie, Frieda, Onagain
and we can see civilization
in its current state inadequate.
Sing us the blues, a wintery one:

'Wuz born, born, born on Saturday night
Seem like that the only day don't turn out right.

Gal Tuesday, my gal left on a Saturday night
Don' seem like she been treatin' me right."

Add to the blues a plain slate gravestone,
Aura and Onagain emblazoned
forever let them slide down through time
past the galaxies that spin just once
every millennium. Oh dear Cass,
how can we even speak or address
you who have lost the hope of the world,
the Child of hope and our own Adam.
We simply do not have the right words.
But we do have the words that are left,
the remnant ballads from the bereft.

Forget the battles of regret,
  Half o'er the Bay of Sorrow.
Retune the harp, restring the net
  For tides that wash Tomorrow.

We sing a lover and his lass
  Now lost within an Echo;
While rhymes persist, their double past
  Resounds in verses hecho

In English, in America
  Who now regard their passing
As losing something magical;
  To know them was a blessing.

FOREWORD

The long poem. Doesn't sound inviting to college students like me, though many classics are that. Vergil, Homer were written to be memorized and recited, so in verse. Also, I never got Whitman, who writes with a shotgun, scattering many words, not choosing one; I much preferred Dickinson's writing with a scalpel. And I never saw why American poets write Me Me Me, about themselves. Surely poets live among the dullest lives, unless like Wilfred Owen or Byron, they die in war, or like Pushkin, in a duel. And they can't write recounting that. (Does putting one's head in an oven add the excitement of a duel?)

As in this intro, my verse show the growth of a poet's mind (a mini-Prelude) leading to parodies. The story features many bit parts—homeless Eddy, writing novels from his car, realtor-poets naming streets (not Swamp Road, but Quail Trail), famous poet Ovid or Angelou, kids' books like *Bomba the Jungle Boy,* then a fly-tying old pervert, or Secretarial Science Frieda, even the dog(gerel) poet named after Wordsworth. The major characters? Onagain, Cassie and poor little Aura.

In grad school I discovered that American poets are still Romantic poets, their subject mostly themselves. But my favorite poets wrote little about themselves: Chaucer, Shakespeare, Moliere, Plautus, Ovid, Martial. Byron was the exception, though the self he wrote about was a stagey performance, somewhat like "Will" onstage in Shakespeare's sonnets. Took me until grad school to prefer Byron to Keats. With my Russian, I found Pushkin developed Byron; this part-African Russian became my model, his satire on the poet Lensky.

Poets I've met: MacLeish, Rolfe Humphries, and then at Minnesota grad school I rode the bus with John Berryman, who lived in Prospect Park down the street from me. After a couple years I would nod to him as he sat near the front, always thanking the bus driver for letting him off (one stop before mine, nearer the tower and tennis courts). Never dared to converse with him beyond, "Pretty cold" (a week never above -10 ° F). A year after I left, he jumped off the long bridge I walked across when I drove, had to park across the Mississippi.

His reading of Dickinson was the best I've heard, but not of his own poetry since he read it drunk. *77 Dream Songs* had come out, but back then I preferred *Berryman's Sonnets*. Before Minnesota, my best college freshman grade was in Russian, so I tried Pushkin in grad school, and ten years later lived next to Boston Symphony violinists from Latvia and the Bolshoi. I came to love Pushkin as the best of both Byron and Wordsworth.

Never expected to write my own longish poem. But I began satirizing what I saw as wrong-headed, self-centered American poetry in the 70s, after the death of my genius friend Tom Weiskel—who, had he lived, would have influenced modern literature. Assistant Professor at Yale at age 26, he died three years later, just as Onnie does in my poem. Heroically, tragically. Once Tom was no longer a dependable parodist of bad writing, I took it on myself.

First place I looked was success. And Fame. One American poet cried all the way to the bank— where he must have laughed. Poet and song-writer: No, not Bob

Zimmerman-Dylan, at U Minnesota just before I (and after Garrison Keilor) got there. Not Dylan, nor John Lennon, though he was their contemporary, seven years older. Rod McKuen. His famous book featured synesthesia, which I knew about from Andrew Marvell and a couple centuries later across the channel, Rimbaud and Baudelaire. McKuen had it, *Listen to the Warm,* his first book.

Reacting to this singer-poet's simplicity, I wrote a few stanzas, avoiding pentameters to force an unforced verse. About the same time I gained Russian neighbors, so I worked on my college freshman language and read Russian intros to Tolstoy and Chekhov (amazed at all the French abstractions they and we both used); and I discovered Pushkin. Frankly, I stole his title character's name, Onegin, casting it satirically, Onagain (but Offagain his twin I omitted).

As opposed to most American poets for two centuries, I searched for poets who ignored themselves, especially themselves as writers. Early writers before printing acted as collectors: Dante apologizes for using his own name late in his *Divina Commedia*; Chaucer gives himself the worst of the *Canterbury Tales,* one the genial Host reacts to, "This maye well be rime doggerel." (Does this make Chaucer the first of our rappers...who all write doggerel.) The Host adds, "Thy drasty rymyng is nat worth a toord!" He also mocks Chaucer's appearance, a small pot-bellied man on his horse, staring shyly at the ground.

Shakespeare apologizes for one of his best plays, *As You Like It,* when the Epilog Rosalind says, "...a good play needs no epilog...What a case am I in then, that am neither a good epilogue nor can insinuate with you in the behalf of a good play!" And he calls himself plain Will in his sonnets, though often punning on volition, will, "So I will pray that thou mayst have thy Will...."(sonn 143).

Nearly a century earlier, Erasmus amuses and shocks us in his school Latin text *Colloquiae*, #IV, the Teen and the Prostitute. She asks why he's grown so modest; he says, he's been to Rome. She, "*That* usually has the opposite effect. He, "No, no, I read a pious author there." "Who?" He, "Erasmus." She, "Erasmus! I've heard he's an arch-heretic... My client said so, a priest."

Now and then I worked and played on my *Parodies* for over a decade before my Pushkin was displaced by Vikram Seth's *The Golden Gate* (1991), a brilliant Russian derivative, which has been diminished—and augmented—by classification as "gay lit," which it is and is not. It holds its own in comparison to Pushkin and his major influence, Byron. I cannot so aspire, but at its best here and there, *Parodies Lost* may bear comparison with my bus-mate Berryman.

From my whole year imitating Dickinson, I did one that should have been hidden in the Manse; written with old ink—Voila! A newly discovered MS. See if you agree, as with my Ashbery and Angelou. This critical poem invites criticism, and if unique, parody.

But I did not expect how *Parodies Lost* ends. The tone changes, the poem revolts. I could not suppress the uprising of my own poem.

www.habitableworlds.com